PCI DSS

A pocket guide

Sixth edition

PCI DSS

A pocket guide

Sixth edition

ALAN CALDER
GERAINT WILLIAMS

IT Governance Publishing

IT Governance Publishing Ltd
Unit 3, Clive Court
Bartholomew's Walk
Cambridgeshire Business Park
Ely, Cambridgeshire
CB7 4EA
United Kingdom
www.itgovernancepublishing.co.uk

© Alan Calder and Nicki Carter 2008, 2011, Alan Calder and Geraint Williams 2013, 2015, 2016, 2019.

The authors have asserted the rights of the authors under the Copyright, Designs and Patents Act, 1988, to be identified as the authors of this work.

First published in the United Kingdom in 2008 by IT Governance Publishing:
ISBN 978-1-90535-664-5

Second edition published in 2011:
ISBN 978-1-84928-172-0

Third edition published in 2013:
ISBN 978-1-84928-554-4

Fourth edition published in 2015:
ISBN: 978-1-84928-781-4

Fifth edition published in 2016:
ISBN: 978-1-84928-843-9

Sixth edition published in 2019:
ISBN: 978-1-78778-162-7

FOREWORD

All target dates for compliance with the PCI DSS have long since passed. The Standard is now on its third version, with the fourth in development with a predicted release date of Q4 2020. It is likely that v3.2.1 will be withdrawn around the end of 2021. Many organisations around the world – particularly those that fall below the top tier of payment card transaction volumes – are not yet compliant.

There are three possible reasons for this.

The first is that, outside a few US states, the PCI DSS has no legal status: it is not a law and does not have the force of law. Enforcement can only be carried out by contractual means, in a competitive payment card marketplace. The UK's Information Commissioner, however, has said that compliance with the PCI DSS shows due diligence in protecting cardholder data, and has effectively imposed it as law through the threat of fines if non-compliant at the time of a breach.[1]

The second is that enforcement is driven by the card payment brands, through the banks that have the commercial relationships with the merchants that are supposed to comply. While enforcement has become more rigorous over the past few years, it is still inconsistent.

The third is that the PCI DSS is extremely prescriptive, and takes a determined one-size-fits-all approach to information security requirements. Compliance is therefore seen as both expensive and bureaucratic.

As a result, many merchants have tried to avoid compliance. However, this is a short-sighted and high-risk stance to adopt – rather like assuming that your business has no exposure to acts

---

[1] *www.out-law.com/page-12147*.

of nature or IT failure and does not, therefore, require a business or IT service continuity plan.

All businesses that accept payment cards are prey for hackers and criminal gangs seeking to steal payment card and individual identity details. Many attacks are highly automated, seeking out website and payment card system vulnerabilities remotely, using increasingly sophisticated tools and techniques. When a vulnerability is discovered, an attack can start – with the management and staff of the target company unaware of what is going on.

Most breaches go undetected for months, and are often found by third parties, such as payment brands conducting fraud checks. When the attack is exposed, the target company faces a harsh and expensive set of repercussions. These range from customer desertion and brand damage to significant penalties and operating requirements imposed by their acquiring bank, including monitoring at a level normally applicable to only the very largest of merchants. Penalties can also include expensive forensic investigation by accredited PCI Forensic Investigators (PFIs), or being made designated entities by the payment brands or the acquirers, requiring an additional level of validation to prove compliance in the future.

The PCI DSS is designed to ensure that merchants are protecting cardholder data effectively. It recognises that not all merchants have the technical understanding to identify the necessary steps and short circuits to avoid danger. All merchants and their service providers should therefore ensure that they comply with the Standard, and that they stay compliant. If the solution cannot be found internally or through the service provider, then training and consultancy is the solution.

Above all else, if every merchant cooperates in the fight against the theft of cardholder data, we might make it easier in the long run for our payment card customers.

ABOUT THE AUTHORS

Alan Calder is a leading author on IT governance and information security issues. He is the CEO of GRC International Group plc, the AIM-listed company that owns IT Governance Ltd – the one-stop shop for books, tools, training and consultancy on governance, risk management and compliance.

Alan is an acknowledged international cyber security guru. He has been involved in the development of a wide range of information security management training courses that have been accredited by the International Board for IT Governance Qualifications (IBITGQ).

He is a frequent media commentator on information security and IT governance issues, and has contributed articles and expert comment to a wide range of trade, national and online news outlets.

Geraint Williams is the CISO for the GRC International Group of companies and a knowledgeable and experienced senior information security consultant and former PCI QSA, with a strong technical background and experience in the PCI DSS and security testing.

Geraint has provided consultancy on implementing the PCI DSS and has conducted audits for a wide range of merchants and service providers as well as penetration testing and vulnerability assessments for various clients. Geraint is the subject matter expert for the IT Governance CISSP Accelerated Training Programme along with the PCI Foundation and Implementer training courses. He has broad technical knowledge of security and IT infrastructure, including high-performance computing and Cloud computing. His certifications include CISSP and PCIP, among others.

ACKNOWLEDGEMENTS

The PCI DSS, copies of which are freely available (although subject to licence) from the PCI Security Standards Council (PCI SSC), is, of course, the PCI SSC's copyright. This pocket guide is not a substitute for acquiring and reading the Standard itself. Every reader of this pocket guide should obtain a copy of the PCI DSS from:
www.pcisecuritystandards.org/document_library.

This pocket guide contains many references to, and summaries of, material that is freely and more comprehensively available on the PCI SSC website and elsewhere. It is intended to be a handy, comprehensive reference tool that contains in one place all the information that anyone dealing with the PCI DSS and related issues might need. It is also a pocket guide, not a comprehensive manual on implementing the Standard.

IT Governance offers dedicated PCI DSS courses at both foundation and implementation levels, allowing businesses to quickly get to grips with PCI DSS requirements.[2]

---

[2] *www.itgovernance.co.uk/shop/category/pci-dss-training-courses.*

CONTENTS

CHAPTER 1: WHAT IS THE PAYMENT CARD INDUSTRY DATA SECURITY STANDARD (PCI DSS)?

The Payment Card Industry Data Security Standard (PCI DSS) was developed by the five founding payment brands of the PCI Security Standards Council (PCI SSC, at *www.pcisecuritystandards.org*): American Express, Discover Financial Services, JCB International, Mastercard and Visa.

The PCI DSS consists of a standardised, industry-wide set of requirements and processes for security management, policies, procedures, network architecture, software design and critical protective measures.

The requirements of the PCI DSS must be met by all organisations (merchants and service providers) that transmit, process or store payment card data, or directly or indirectly affect the security of cardholder data. If an organisation uses a third party to manage cardholder data, it has a responsibility to ensure that the third party is compliant with the PCI DSS.

The PCI DSS (sometimes referred to as a compliance standard) is not a law. It is a contractual obligation applied and enforced – by means of fines or other restrictions – directly by the payment providers themselves.

The currently applicable version of the PCI DSS, since May 2018, is version 3.2.1; subject to licence, it can be freely downloaded.[3] It is published and controlled by the PCI SSC on behalf of its five founding members.

In June 2015, the PCI SSC introduced the concept of 'designated entities'. These are high-risk entities that can be prescribed a set of supplemental validation requirements to demonstrate ongoing security efforts to protect payments.

---

[3] *www.pcisecuritystandards.org/document_library*.

The SSC also defines qualifications for Qualified Security Assessors (QSAs), Internal Security Assessors (ISAs), PCI Forensic Investigators (PFIs), PCI Professionals (PCIPs), Qualified Integrators and Resellers (QIRs) and Approved Scanning Vendors (ASVs). It trains, tests, certifies and runs quality assurance programmes for these certifications.

The PCI DSS is a set of 12 requirements that are imposed on merchants and other related parties. These requirements are described later in this pocket guide.

Key definitions[4] and acronyms in the PCI DSS

Acquirer – a bank that acquires merchants – i.e. the bank with which you have your e-commerce bank account.

Payment brand – Visa, Mastercard, American Express, Discover, JCB.

Merchant – sells products to cardholders.

Service provider – a business entity that is directly or indirectly involved in the processing, storage, transmission and switching of cardholder data. This includes companies that provide services to merchants, service providers, or members that control or could impact the security of cardholder data.

Service providers include:

- Third-party processors (TPPs), which process payment card transactions (including payment gateways); and

- Data storage entities (DSEs), which store or transmit payment card data.

Primary account number (PAN) – the up-to-19-digit payment card number.

---

[4] There is a formal English glossary available at *www.pcisecuritystandards.org/document_library*.

1: What is the Payment Card Industry Data Security Standard (PCI DSS)?

Qualified Security Assessor (QSA) – someone who is trained and certified to carry out PCI DSS compliance assessments.

Internal Security Assessor (ISA) – someone who is trained and certified to conduct internal security assessments.

Approved Scanning Vendor (ASV) – an organisation that is approved as competent to carry out the security scans required by the PCI DSS.

PCI Forensic Investigator (PFI) – an individual trained and certified to investigate and contain information security breaches involving cardholder data.

CHAPTER 2: RECENT CARDHOLDER BREACHES

E-commerce breaches

There have been a number of high-profile attacks by the threat group Magecart, including major breaches of British Airways and Ticketmaster UK. In both incidents, a script was used to intercept cardholders' details as they entered them into a browser on the cardholders' own machines.

- In the British Airways breach, Magecart managed to get a modified script onto the web server and application itself.

- In the case of Ticketmaster UK, Magecart managed to get a substitute script onto a service provider's server. The malicious script was then called from the Ticketmaster website and captured card details.

In the case of British Airways, server and application access controls should have prevented the script from being modified, and change detection should have recognised that the script had been changed. Ticketmaster, meanwhile, should have ensured that the service provider was PCI DSS compliant, as the script was being called from the web page that hosted payment entry.

Hospitality industry

Criminal hackers have for several years targeted the point-of-sale (POS) equipment used to take payments in order to steal cardholder data, breaching numerous restaurant and hotel chains.

- Two million customer credit cards were stolen between May 2018 and March 2019 from more than 100 restaurants belonging to Earl Enterprises. The restaurants, which include Planet Hollywood, Buca di Beppo, and Earl of Sandwich, had their POS terminals infected with malware; the stolen credit card numbers were on sale less than a month later.

- Malware was found on payment processing servers used at restaurants and bars in the InterContinental Hotels Group in 2017. Stolen data included cardholder names, card numbers, expiration dates and internal verification codes.

- US coffee chain Caribou Coffee announced a security breach after it discovered unauthorised access to its POS systems between 28 August and 3 December 2018. 239 of its 603 stores were impacted – amounting to roughly 40% of its sites.

In these cases, and many more, isolating the cardholder data environment (CDE) from the rest of the organisation's network and implementing strong access controls would have helped protect cardholder data.

CHAPTER 3: WHAT IS THE SCOPE OF THE PCI DSS?

The PCI DSS is applicable if you store, process or transmit cardholder data, or if you are responsible for third parties that store, process or transmit cardholder data. It also applies if you are involved with or can affect the security of the storage, processing or transmission of cardholder data. The cardholder data environment (CDE) is any network or environment that possesses cardholder data or sensitive authentication data. It does *not* apply to your organisation if primary account numbers (PANs) are not stored, processed or transmitted. The PCI DSS applies to any type of media on which card data may be held – this includes not only hard disk drives, floppy disks, magnetic tape and back-up media, but also printed or handwritten credit and debit card receipts where the full card number is printed. These receipts are sometimes held by merchants as a paper record of the transaction and may be used for voucher recovery purposes or as evidence of the transaction if the acquirer issues a request for information (RFI). If the card number is recorded in full, the record is subject to the same security requirements as electronic copies, and must be stored securely.

Retailers must also secure all other areas where card details may be stored, processed or transmitted. Electronic point-of-sale (EPOS) systems are worthy of particular note. While newer EPOS systems store card details securely, many older ones do not. If the equipment does not store it securely, or there is uncertainty about whether it is secure, retailers should take firmer measures to protect the equipment, or upgrade to equipment that meets PCI DSS standards.

The PCI DSS applies to all processes, people and technology, and all system components, including network components, servers or applications that are included in or connected to the CDE, and those that can affect the security of the cardholder data. It also applies to telephone recording technology used by call centres that accept payment card transactions. Online shopping carts and payment processing facilities are examples of applications to which the PCI DSS applies (also see Chapter 13 on the Payment Application Data Security Standard (PA-DSS)).

While not a specific requirement, the PCI DSS strongly recommends that any merchant or service provider reduces the scope of its CDE. This reduces the cost and complexity of both the initial assessment and the maintenance of PCI controls. Reducing the scope is typically achieved by reducing the number of systems and processes that are involved with cardholder data and isolating (network segmenting) the CDE. Given the complexity of modern IT networks and applications, we advise seeking the advice of a qualified PCI DSS consultant before completing this activity.

CHAPTER 4: COMPLIANCE AND COMPLIANCE PROGRAMMES

Payment brands enforce the compliance process through contractual means, including higher processing fees, fines and financial penalties for non-compliance. These penalties can be applied monthly during the remediation process, and additional fines can be levied for breaches.

What are the consequences to my business if I do not comply with the PCI DSS?

"The PCI Security Standards Council encourages all businesses that store payment account data to comply with the PCI DSS to help lower their brand and financial risks associated with account payment data compromises. The PCI Security Standards Council does not manage compliance programs and does not impose any consequences for non-compliance. Individual payment brands, however, may have their own compliance initiatives, including financial or operational consequences to certain businesses that are not compliant."[5]

This means that each payment provider will take whatever action it thinks it can make stick, commercially, to enforce the PCI DSS. There are no standardised penalties across all the payment brands, and the PCI SSC has no plans to create any. Because individual payment brands have their own compliance initiatives, each requires separate evidence of compliance. Given that the original dates for compliance have now all passed, each brand is likely to set different dates for different levels and different entities to demonstrate compliance. The acquiring bank is usually the best channel through which to discuss compliance deadlines and penalties, which are all imposed by means of the payment brand/acquiring bank's contract with the merchant.

---

[5] FAQ from the PCI DSS website, *www.pcisecuritystandards.org/faqs*.

While the PCI DSS is a common standard, each payment brand has its own compliance programme. Note that there are regional variations for Visa (e.g. USA and Europe), while Mastercard has a single global standard, and that acquiring banks – not the payment brands – are usually responsible for enforcement. All detailed compliance enquiries should therefore be directed to your acquiring bank. Detailed below are the websites for the PCI DSS compliance programmes for each of the five founding members of the PCI SSC, which will give some guidance on the compliance actions that might be expected in respect of each of the payment brands:

Contact details for the payment brands are kept on the PCI SSC website and regularly updated as part of the FAQ section[6].

American Express

Website: *https://merchant-channel.americanexpress.com/merchant/en_US/data-security*

Email: *AmericanExpressCompliance@trustwave.com*

Discover

Website: *https://www.discoverglobalnetwork.com/en-us/*

For questions about the Discover Information Security & Compliance (DISC) Program:

https://www.discoverglobalnetwork.com/en-us/business-resources/fraud-security/pci-rules-regulations/

Email: *DISCCompliance@discover.com*

JCB

Website: *https://www.global.jcb/en/products/security/data-security-program/*

---

[6] *www.pcisecuritystandards.org/faqs* Article number 1142 *How do I contact the payment card brands?*

Email: *riskmanagement@jcbati.com*

Mastercard

Website: *https://www.mastercard.us/en-us/merchants/safety-security/security-recommendations/site-data-protection-PCI.html*

Email: *sdp@mastercard.com*

Visa – Canada, US, Latin America and the Caribbean

Website: *https://usa.visa.com/support/small-business/security-compliance.html?ep=v_sym_cisp*

Email: *cisp@visa.com*

Visa Europe

Website: *https://www.visa.co.uk/about-visa/visa-in-europe.html*

Email: *datasecuritystandards@visa.com* (for member and merchant requirements)

Email: *pcidsseurope@visa.com* (for service provider requirements)

Visa – Asia Pacific, Central Europe, Middle East and Africa

For merchant requirements

Website: *https://www.visa.com.sg/support/small-business/security-compliance.html*

Email: *vpssais@visa.com*

For service provider requirements

Website: *https://www.visa.com.sg/partner-with-us/pci-dss-compliance-information.html*

Email: *pciagents@visa.com*

CHAPTER 5: CONSEQUENCES OF A BREACH

The consequences of a data security breach are likely to be proportionate to the seriousness of the breach and the extent to which the merchant or service provider is able to demonstrate prior compliance with the PCI DSS. The penalties can be any or all of the following:

- A significant cost for a forensic investigation.
- The merchant automatically becoming a level 1 merchant (i.e. yearly on-site audits).
- A possible charge by issuer(s) to acquirer(s) for card reissue, which may be passed on to the merchant.
- The merchant may lose its ability to accept payment cards.
- Transaction costs may be increased.
- Service providers may be removed from listings by the payment brands.
- Merchants or service providers may become designated entities and subject to additional validation requirements.

For level 1 merchants, the combination of fines, litigation and brand damage is significant; for non-level 1 merchants, the consequences of a breach can be just as serious.

CHAPTER 6: HOW DO YOU COMPLY WITH THE REQUIREMENTS OF THE STANDARD?

All organisations must comply with the PCI DSS. There are two options for demonstrating compliance: an annual on-site security audit by a QSA or ISA and the submission of four passing quarterly network scans by an ASV, or completion of a Self-Assessment Questionnaire (SAQ) and the submission of four passing quarterly network scans. Which option applies is determined by an organisation's transaction volume and whether or not it has previously suffered a security breach.

The major global payment brands require that every entity – including financial institutions, merchants and service providers – that stores, processes or transmits payment card data, in every channel – including catalogue and online retailers, as well as bricks-and-mortar businesses – must comply with the PCI DSS.

Merchant PCI DSS compliance criteria

Compliance requirements are dependent on a merchant's activity level. There are four levels, based on the annual number of credit/debit card transactions. While payment brands determine the compliance levels for their own brands, acquirers are usually responsible for determining the compliance validation requirement levels of their merchants. The compliance levels are based on the following table and usually refer to the number of transactions of each payment brand in a year. Whether or not transaction volume applies only to e-commerce transactions or to payments processed through all channels is decided separately by each payment brand but, in general, all transactions are included.

Table 1: Merchant PCI DSS Compliance Levels

Level 1 criteria:

American Express

2.5 million American Express card transactions or more per year.

Any merchant that has had a data incident.

Any merchant that American Express otherwise deems a level 1.

Visa

Merchants processing more than 6 million Visa transactions per year via all channels.

Global merchants identified as level 1 by any Visa region.

Mastercard

Any merchant having more than 6 million total combined Mastercard and Maestro transactions per year.

Any merchant that has suffered a hack or an attack that resulted in an account data compromise.

Any merchant meeting Visa's level 1 criteria.

Any merchant that Mastercard determines should meet the level 1 merchant requirements to minimise risk to the system.

Discover

All merchants processing more than 6 million card transactions per year on the Discover network.

Any merchant that Discover determines should meet the level 1 compliance validation and reporting requirements.

All merchants required by another payment brand or acquirer to validate and report their compliance as a level 1 merchant.

JCB

1 million JCB transactions or more per year for merchants (excluding Internet payment service providers (IPSPs)).

All IPSPs regardless of volume.

Level 1 validation requirements:

Annual on-site audit by a QSA or ISA, passing ASV scans and submitting a Report on Compliance (RoC).

Level 2 criteria:

American Express

50,000 to 2.5 million American Express card transactions per year.

Visa/Mastercard/Discover

Merchants processing 1 to 6 million transactions per year, across all of the brand's channels.

JCB

Fewer than 1 million JCB transactions per year for merchants (excluding IPSPs).

Level 2 validation requirements:

Annual SAQ, passing a quarterly scan by an ASV.

In addition to passing quarterly network scans by an ASV, Mastercard requires either an annual on-site audit by a QSA at the merchant's discretion, or an annual self-assessment by an ISA.

Quarterly network scans by an ASV are only a requirement on some SAQ forms; check the requirements with the payment brand compliance programmes.

Level 3 criteria:

American Express (designated)

Fewer than 50,000 American Express card transactions per year and has been designated by American Express as being required to submit validation documents. American Express will contact these designated merchants and provide them with details for reporting their security status by submitting PCI validation documents.

American Express

Fewer than 50,000 American Express card transactions per year (recommended to submit an SAQ and ASV scans).

Visa

Merchants processing 20,000 to 1 million Visa e-commerce transactions per year, across all of the brand's channels.

Mastercard

Merchants processing 20,000 to 1 million Mastercard and Maestro e-commerce transactions per year.

Any merchant meeting the level 3 criteria of Visa.

Discover

All other merchants.

Level 3 validation requirements:

Quarterly scan by an ASV.

Annual SAQ.

Level 4 criteria:

American Express

Called 'Level EMV'; 50,000 or more American Express transactions per year, with at least 75% made on an EMV-enabled terminal.

Visa

E-commerce merchants processing fewer than 20,000 Visa e-commerce transactions annually.

Non e-commerce merchants processing up to one million Visa transactions annually.

Mastercard/Discover

All other merchants.

Level 4 validation requirements:

Annual SAQ.

Quarterly scan by an ASV (may be recommended or required, depending on acquirer compliance criteria).

Special designations:

American Express (EMV)

50,000 or more American Express chip-enabled card transactions per year with at least 75% made on an EMV-enabled (chip-enabled) terminal capable of processing contact and contactless American Express transactions.

American Express (EMV) validation requirements

Annual EMV Attestation (AEA) (required).

The PCI Council is clear that PCI DSS compliance is required even if there is only one payment card transaction per year.

Service provider PCI DSS compliance criteria

A service provider is an organisation involved in the processing, storage and transmission of cardholder data, and/or protecting the security of cardholder data, but is not a merchant or a card brand member. Hosting providers and others providing services to merchants would also fall into this category.

Service provider compliance requirements are defined by the payment brands. Visa, Mastercard and American Express categorise service providers according to transaction volume and/or type of service provider. In comparison with the four levels of merchant compliance criteria, there are only two for service providers.

Table 2: Service Provider PCI DSS Compliance Levels

Level 1 criteria: *American Express*   2.5 million American Express card transactions or more per year, or any other service provider that American Express otherwise deems a level 1 service provider.   *Visa*   VisaNet processors or any service provider that stores, processes and/or transmits more than 300,000 Visa transactions annually.   *Mastercard*   All Third Party Processors (TPPs)   All Staged Digital Wallet Operators (SDWOs)   All Digital Activity Service Providers (DASPs)   All Token Service Providers (TSPs)   All 3-D Secure Service Providers (3-DSSPs)

All Data Storage Entities (DSEs) and Payment Facilitators (PFs) with more than 300,000 total combined Mastercard and Maestro transactions annually.

Discover

All service providers that store, process and/or transmit more than 300,000 Discover card transactions per year.

Any service provider that Discover, at its sole discretion, determines should meet the level 1 compliance validation and reporting requirements.

JCB

All TPPs with 1 million or more transactions.

Level 1 validation requirements:

Visa, Mastercard and American Express

Annual on-site review by a QSA.

Quarterly network scan by an ASV.

Level 2 criteria:

American Express

Fewer than 2.5 million transactions.

Visa

Any service provider that stores, processes and/or transmits fewer than 300,000 Visa transactions annually.

Mastercard

All DSEs and PFs with 300,000 or fewer total combined Mastercard and Maestro transactions annually.

All Terminal Servicers (TSs).

Discover

All service providers that store, process and/or transmit fewer than 300,000 Discover card transactions per year.

JCB

All TPPs with fewer than 1 million transactions.

Level 2 validation requirements:

Visa, Mastercard and American Express

Annual SAQ. Quarterly network scan by an ASV.

Designated entities will have to complete an additional set of requirements within an appendix to the main PCI DSS. An acquirer or payment brand will determine if an organisation requires additional validation. As designated entities, it is very likely they will also be made a level 1 merchant or service provider.

Role of service providers

Many service providers deliver payment services directly to merchants using a variety of online and physical technologies. These services include online payment gateways, traditional document processing facilities and shared hosting server and application providers. The PCI DSS asks that shared hosting providers ensure compliance with additional requirements, which include protecting each merchant's hosted individual CDE, ensuring the availability of audit trails and allowing forensic investigation if required. To achieve compliance, a merchant must ensure that any service provider it uses is PCI DSS compliant.

Service providers that have an indirect connection with the storage, processing or transmission of cardholder data – such as an IT support company that manages the firewalls in the perimeter of the CDE and hence can affect the inbound and outbound traffic – are also required to be PCI DSS compliant.

Service providers demonstrate their compliance with the PCI DSS with criteria as outlined in Table 2. The PCI DSS recommends that, in addition to achieving compliance with the requirements of the Standard, service providers should also provide supporting evidence (via an AoC) to prove to merchants that they are compliant. Service providers and merchants must agree in writing which aspects of the PCI DSS requirements the service provider is responsible for ensuring compliance with and which the merchant is responsible for. Merchants must maintain a list of service providers and the compliant services they provide.

Service providers can register their compliance with the card brands and be listed on their websites.

Online payment gateways

We strongly recommend that merchants that sell their products or services online use a third-party payment gateway service that is fully PCI compliant. These services are available from PayPal, Sage Pay, Stripe, WorldPay, HSBC Secure ePayments and Barclays ePDQ. For smaller e-commerce business, outsourcing to a payment gateway service is a cost-effective way of ensuring PCI compliance.

Please note that such a merchant (likely to be level 3 or 4) will be required to complete the relevant SAQ and submit the results of a quarterly scan by an ASV. The SAQ document required will be SAQ A for those who have a fully outsourced e-commerce platform, SAQ A-EP for those who use only partially outsourced e-commerce platforms, or SAQ C-VT, which applies to merchants that use web-based virtual terminals to manually enter payment card information. See Chapter 10, Table 3 for further information.

A number of these service providers provide tools and support for merchants to complete and submit PCI DSS compliance documentation. In some cases, the service provider, especially if they are also the merchant acquiring bank, will automate the process and complete the documentation for the merchant providing the merchant has implemented the solution in exactly the way the service provider has stated.

CHAPTER 7: MAINTAINING COMPLIANCE

Once an organisation has achieved compliance with the PCI DSS, it must maintain its level of compliance. This means being aware of any changes to the PCI DSS itself (the latest version was released in May 2018), as well as maintaining the PCI DSS security environment.

Any changes to in-scope systems, processes and technologies must be implemented in a PCI DSS-compliant manner, and their effect on compliance assessed and recorded. If it is significant change, all requirements that are mandatory to be revaluated after a significant change must be completed and the result recorded.

All PCI DSS processes must be followed and maintained at all times throughout the period between recertifications.

The PCI SSC makes the point this way: technically, it is true that, if you've completed an SAQ, you're compliant – "for that particular moment in time when the Self-Assessment Questionnaire and associated vulnerability scan (if applicable) is completed. After that moment, only a post-breach forensic analysis can prove PCI compliance. But a bad system change can make you non-compliant in an instant. True security of cardholder data requires non-stop assessment and remediation to ensure that likelihood of a breach is kept as low as possible."[7]

Version 3.2 of the PCI DSS incorporated the requirements for designated entities supplemental validation (DESV) as an appendix to the Standard called Appendix A3. Although the DESV/Appendix A3 is for those entities that have been designated, the PCI SSC recommends that the controls be used to complement any entity's PCI DSS compliance efforts, and all

---

[7]

www.pcisecuritystandards.org/documents/pciscc_ten_common_myths. pdf (Myth 8).

entities are encouraged to follow them as a best practice, even if they are not required to validate.

Version 3.2.1 of the PCI DSS removed dated requirements as all dates have now passed and all requirements are now mandatory. It also clarified some of the controls following feedback.

CHAPTER 8: PCI DSS – THE STANDARD

The PCI DSS has 12 requirements, organised into 6 control objectives. Please note that this pocket guide is no substitute for obtaining your own copy of the Standard, which is freely downloadable:
www.pcisecuritystandards.org/security_standards/documents.php.

PCI DSS version 1.0 was originally published in January 2005, and subsequently updated to version 1.1 in September 2006 and version 1.2 in October 2008. PCI DSS version 2.0 was released on 28 October 2010, and version 3.0 was published on 7 November 2013, with version 3.1 released in April 2015 and 3.2 in April 2016. The current iteration, version 3.2.1, was released May 2018.

With the release of PCI DSS version 2.0, the PCI SSC introduced a three-year lifecycle for standards development. This ensures a gradual and phased introduction of new versions, and helps prevent organisations from becoming non-compliant when a new version is published.

Version 3.0 of the PCI DSS introduces more flexibility in implementing the Standard's requirements, and increases the focus on education, awareness and security as a shared responsibility.

Version 3.1 is an out-of-band update created in response to the repeated vulnerabilities discovered in the SSL security protocol in early 2015. It removes SSL and early versions of TLS as secure technologies, and dictates that they are replaced with TLS 1.2 and beyond, or IPsec.

Since version 3.1, however, the PCI SSC has abandoned the three-year cycle in favour of more frequent incremental updates to help the Standard keep up with a faster pace of change within the security industry.

Version 3.2 was an incremental update introducing business-as-usual (BAU) requirements. Organisations have typically focused on the annual assessment rather than continually managing their compliance state. Compliance is often only at its peak following the annual assessment, and trails off over time. Version 3.2 targets service providers by adding guidance for maintaining card security as part of their BAU activities.

Appendix A3 has been added to state the requirements for designated entities, and Appendix A2 has been added to provide clear guidance on transitioning from using SSL and early TLS, with extended timescales provided for transitions supported by formal risk assessments and mitigation plans.

The 6 control objectives and 12 PCI DSS requirements that address these are as follows:

Build and maintain a secure network and systems

Requirement 1: Install and maintain a firewall configuration to protect cardholder data.

Requirement 2: Do not use vendor-supplied defaults for system passwords and other security parameters.

Protect cardholder data

Requirement 3: Protect stored cardholder data.

Requirement 4: Encrypt transmission of cardholder data across open, public networks.

Maintain a vulnerability management programme

Requirement 5: Protect all systems against malware and regularly update anti-virus software or programs.

Requirement 6: Develop and maintain secure systems and applications.

Implement strong access control measures

***Requirement 7*:** Restrict access to cardholder data by business need-to-know.

***Requirement 8*:** Identify and authenticate access to system components.

Requirement 9: Restrict physical access to cardholder data.

Regularly monitor and test networks

***Requirement 10*:** Track and monitor all access to network resources and cardholder data.

***Requirement 11*:** Regularly test security systems and processes.

Maintain an information security policy

***Requirement 12*:** Maintain a policy that addresses information security for all personnel.

CHAPTER 9: ASPECTS OF PCI DSS COMPLIANCE

Requirement 1 (Install and maintain a firewall configuration to protect cardholder data)

- Establish and implement firewall and router configuration standards.
- Build firewall and router configurations that restrict connections between untrusted networks and any system components in the cardholder data environment.
- Prohibit direct public access between the Internet and any system component in the cardholder data environment.
- Install personal firewall software on any mobile and/or employee-owned devices that connect to the Internet when outside the network.
- Ensure that security policies and operational procedures for managing firewalls are documented, in use, and known to all affected parties.
- Maintain current network and data flow diagrams.

Requirement 2 (Do not use vendor-supplied defaults for system passwords and other security parameters)

- Always change vendor-supplied defaults and remove or disable unnecessary default accounts before installing a system on the network.
- Develop configuration standards for all system components. Ensure that these standards address all known security vulnerabilities and are consistent with industry-accepted system hardening standards.
- Encrypt all non-console administrative access using strong cryptography. Use technologies such as SSH, VPN, or TLS for web-based management and other non-console administrative access.
- Maintain an inventory of system components that are in scope for the PCI DSS.

- Ensure that security policies and operational procedures for managing vendor defaults and other security parameters are documented, in use, and known to all affected parties.
- Shared hosting providers must protect each entity's hosted environment and cardholder data.

Requirement 3 (Protect stored cardholder data)

- Keep cardholder data storage to a minimum by implementing data retention and disposal policies, procedures and processes.
- Do not store sensitive authentication data after authorisation (even if encrypted). If sensitive authentication data is received, render all data unrecoverable upon completion of the authorisation process.
- Mask PAN when displayed (the first six and last four digits, at maximum), such that only personnel with a legitimate business need can see the full PAN.
- Render PAN unreadable anywhere it is stored (including on portable digital media, backup media, and in logs).
- Document and implement procedures to protect keys used to secure stored cardholder data against disclosure and misuse.
- Fully document and implement all key-management processes and procedures for cryptographic keys used for encryption of cardholder data.
- Ensure that security policies and operational procedures for protecting stored cardholder data are documented, in use, and known to all affected parties.
- Service providers must maintain and detail their cryptographic architecture, if implemented.

Requirement 4 (Encrypt transmission of cardholder data across open, public networks)

- Use strong cryptography and security protocols (for example, TLS, IPsec, SSH, etc.) to safeguard sensitive cardholder data during transmission over open, public networks.

- Never send unprotected PANs by end-user messaging technologies (for example, email, instant messaging, chat etc.).
- Ensure that security policies and operational procedures for encrypting transmissions of cardholder data are documented, in use, and known to all affected parties.

Requirement 5 (Protect all systems against malware and regularly update anti-virus software or programs)

- Deploy antivirus software on all systems commonly affected by malicious software. (If there is malware targeting a particular platform and there is anti-malware software available it should be deployed.)
- Ensure that all antivirus mechanisms are maintained.
- Ensure that antivirus mechanisms are actively running and cannot be disabled or altered by users, unless specifically authorised by management on a case-by-case basis for a limited time period.
- Ensure that security policies and operational procedures for protecting systems against malware are documented, in use, and known to all affected parties.

Requirement 6 (Develop and maintain secure systems and applications)

- Establish a process to identify security vulnerabilities, using reputable outside sources for security vulnerability information, and assign a risk ranking.
- Ensure that all system components and software are protected from known vulnerabilities by installing applicable vendor-supplied security patches. Install critical security patches within one month of release.
- Develop internal and external software applications securely (including web-based administrative access to applications).

- Follow change control processes and procedures for all changes to system components.
- Address common coding vulnerabilities in software development processes.
- For public-facing web applications, address new threats and vulnerabilities on an ongoing basis and ensure these applications are protected against known attacks.
- Ensure that security policies and operational procedures for developing and maintaining secure systems and applications are documented, in use, and known to all affected parties.
- Upon completion of a significant change, all relevant PCI DSS requirements must be implemented on all new or changed systems and networks, and documentation updated as applicable.

Requirement 7 (Restrict access to cardholder data by business need-to-know)

- Limit access to system components and cardholder data to only those individuals whose job requires such access.
- Establish an access control system for systems components that restricts access based on a user's need to know, and is set to "deny all" unless specifically allowed.
- Ensure that security policies and operational procedures for restricting access to cardholder data are documented, in use, and known to all affected parties.

Requirement 8 (Identify and authenticate access to system components)

- Define and implement policies and procedures to ensure proper user identification management for non-consumer users and administrators on all system components.
- In addition to assigning a unique ID, ensure proper user-authentication management for non-consumer users and administrators on all system components.
- Incorporate multi-factor authentication for remote network access originating from outside the network by

personnel (including users and administrators) and all third parties, (including vendor access for support or maintenance),

- Implement multi-factor authentication for all administration-level access to any components within the CDE.
- Document and communicate authentication procedures and policies.
- Do not use group, shared or generic IDs, passwords, or other authentication methods.
- Where other authentication mechanisms are used (for example, physical or logical security tokens, smart cards, certificates etc.), use of these mechanisms must be assigned to an individual account and only the intended account can use that mechanism.
- All access to any database containing cardholder data (including access by applications, administrators, and all other users) is restricted.
- Ensure that security policies and operational procedures for identification and authentication are documented, in use, and known to all affected parties.
- Additional requirement for service providers: service providers must implement and maintain a system for identification and response to failures in security controls, such as logging and segmentation.

Requirement 9 (Restrict physical access to cardholder data)

- Use appropriate facility entry controls to limit and monitor physical access to systems in the cardholder data environment.
- Develop procedures to easily distinguish between onsite personnel and visitors.
- Control physical access for onsite personnel to the sensitive areas.
- Implement procedures to identify and authorise visitors.
- Physically secure all media.
- Maintain strict control over the internal or external distribution of any kind of media

- Maintain strict control over the storage and accessibility of media.
- Destroy media when it is no longer needed for business or legal reasons.
- Protect devices that capture payment card data via direct physical interaction with the card from tampering and substitution.
- Ensure that security policies and operational procedures for restricting physical access to cardholder data are documented, in use, and known to all affected parties.

Requirement 10 (Track and monitor all access to network resources and cardholder data)

- Implement audit trails to link all access to system components to each individual user.
- Implement automated audit trails for all system components to reconstruct events,
- create an audit trail for all system components for each event,
- Using time-synchronisation technology, synchronise all critical system clocks and times and ensure that the following is implemented for acquiring, distributing and storing time.
- Secure audit trails so they cannot be altered.
- Review logs and security events for all system components to identify anomalies or suspicious activity.
- Retain audit trail history for at least one year, with a minimum of three months immediately available for analysis.
- Ensure that security policies and operational procedures for monitoring all access to network resources and cardholder data are documented, in use, and known to all affected parties.
- Additional requirement for service providers only: Implement a process for the timely detection and reporting of failures of critical security control systems.

- Additional requirement for service providers only: Respond to failures of any critical security controls in a timely manner

Requirement 11 (Regularly test security systems and processes)

- Implement processes to test for the presence of wireless access points (802.11), and detect and identify all authorised and unauthorised wireless access points on a quarterly basis.
- Maintain an inventory of authorized wireless access points including a documented business justification.
- Run internal and external network vulnerability scans at least quarterly and after any significant change in the network.
- Implement a methodology for penetration testing.
- Perform internal and external penetration testing at least annually.
- If segmentation is used to isolate the CDE from other networks, perform penetration tests at least annually and after any changes to segmentation controls/methods to verify that the segmentation methods are operational and effective, and isolate all out-of-scope systems from systems in the CDE
- Additional requirement for service providers: perform penetration testing on internal segmentation systems at least every six months.
- Use intrusion-detection and/or intrusion-prevention techniques to detect and/or prevent intrusions into the network.
- Deploy a change-detection mechanism to alert personnel to unauthorised modification of critical system files, configuration files, or content files; and configure the software to perform critical file comparisons at least weekly.
- Ensure that security policies and operational procedures for security monitoring and testing are documented, in use, and known to all affected parties.

Requirement 12 (Maintain a policy that addresses information security for all personnel)

- Establish, publish, maintain and disseminate a security policy, and review and update annually.
- Implement a risk assessment process, and review and update annually.
- Develop usage policies for critical technologies and define proper use of these technologies.
- Ensure that the security policy and procedures clearly define information security responsibilities for all personnel.
- Assign to an individual or team information security management responsibilities.
- Implement a formal security awareness programme to make all personnel aware of the importance of cardholder data security.
- Screen potential personnel prior to hire to minimise the risk of attacks from internal sources.
- Maintain and implement policies and procedures to manage service providers with whom cardholder data is shared, or that could affect the security of cardholder data.
- Additional requirement for service providers: service providers must establish a charter to define executive responsibility for the protection of cardholder data and maintenance of PCI DSS compliance.
- Additional requirement for service providers: Service providers acknowledge in writing to customers that they are responsible for the security of cardholder data the service provider possesses or otherwise stores, processes or transmits on behalf of the customer, or to the extent that they could impact the security of the customer's cardholder data environment.
- Additional requirement for service providers: service providers must perform quarterly reviews of staff adherence to security policies and operational procedures.
- Implement an incident response plan. Be prepared to respond immediately to a system breach.

When an organisation is unable to meet the strict requirements of the PCI DSS owing to legitimate or documented business constraints, it is permissible to submit a number of alternative measures. These measures are known as compensating controls, and must fully mitigate the risks associated with the requirements and meet the criteria as defined in PCI DSS Appendix B: Compensating Controls. On an annual basis, any compensating controls must be documented, reviewed and validated by the assessor and included with the RoC submission.

It is also possible for an organisation to mark requirements as 'not applicable' if sufficient justification for the non-applicability can be provided. Further details on this are provided in the reporting instructions within the RoC and SAQ.

CHAPTER 10: THE PCI SELF-ASSESSMENT QUESTIONNAIRE (SAQ)

The PCI DSS SAQ is a validation tool developed by the PCI SSC to assist merchants and service providers in self-evaluating their compliance with the PCI DSS.

All merchants and their service providers are required to comply with the PCI DSS in its entirety and, if they are eligible for self-assessment, to attest that they comply by using the standard Attestation of Compliance (AoC) document. New SAQs and AoCs were released in 2018 to meet the requirements of version 3.2.1 of the PCI DSS.

In most recent versions of the questionnaire, there were nine validation categories (*see Table 3*), each of which can be downloaded from:
www.pcisecuritystandards.org/document_library.

Table 3: Self-Assessment Questionnaire Validation Categories

SAQ validation type	Description
A	Card-not-present (e-commerce or mail/telephone order) merchants that outsource all cardholder functions and have no direct control over storing, processing or transmitting cardholder data. All payment pages originate from third parties. This never applies to face-to-face merchants.
A-EP	Partially outsourced e-commerce merchants, using a third-party website for payment processing. The merchant's

	website only controls how cardholder data is redirected to a third-party payment processor. No electronic storage, processing or transmission of CHD. Only applies to e-commerce channels.
B	Imprint only or standalone, dial-out (via a phone line) terminal merchants. No transmission of cardholder data over data networks, no electronic storage of CHD. Not applicable to e-commerce channels.
B-IP	Merchants with standalone IP-connected, PTS-approved terminals, the only transmission is from the terminal to the payment processor (isolated connection), no electronic storage of cardholder data. Not applicable to e-commerce channels.
C	Merchants with payment applications connected to the Internet, but isolated from the rest of the environment. The physical location of the POS is not connected to other locations (single LAN only). No electronic storage of cardholder data. Not applicable to e-commerce channels.
C-VT	Merchants with web-based virtual payment terminals in which the virtual terminal system is isolated from the rest of the environment. No attached card readers and no electronic storage of cardholder data. Not applicable to e-commerce channels.
D (Merchants)	All other SAQ-eligible merchants that do not meet the criteria for any other SAQ.
D (Service Providers)	All SAQ-eligible service providers.

| P2PE-HW | Merchants using hardware payment terminals in a PCI-listed P2PE solution. No electronic cardholder data storage, no electronic processing or transmission of cardholder data outside of the P2PE solution. Not applicable to e-commerce channels. |

CHAPTER 11: PROCEDURES AND QUALIFICATIONS

The PCI SSC mandates the procedures that must be followed in conducting audits and in carrying out scanning procedures. It also lays down specific requirements for qualification as a QSA or an ASV.

Qualification Requirements for Qualified Security Assessors (QSA) v3.0

https://www.pcisecuritystandards.org/documents/QSA_Qualific ation_Requirements_v3_0.pdf

To be recognised as a QSA by the PCI SSC, QSAs must meet or exceed the requirements described in the above document and must also execute the QSA Agreement in Appendix A with the PCI Council. Clients can provide feedback on the effectiveness of the QSA.

QSA Feedback Form

https://www.pcisecuritystandards.org/assessors_and_solutions/ qualified_security_assessors_feedback

QSA feedback is completed online.

PCI DSS Qualified Security Assessors

https://www.pcisecuritystandards.org/assessors_and_solutions/ qualified_security_assessors

This list, which is updated regularly, contains contact details for all QSAs, together with information about the markets they serve. Alternatively, you can look up individual assessors in the PSI SSC's database.

ASV Qualification Requirements v 3.0

https://www.pcisecuritystandards.org/documents/ASV_Qualific ation_Requirements_v3.0.pdf

Recognition as an ASV by the PCI Council requires the ASV, its employees and its scanning solution to meet or exceed the requirements described above and to execute the 'PCI ASV Compliance Test Agreement' set out below with the PCI Council. The companies that qualify are then identified on the PCI SSC's ASV list on its website.

Approved Scanning Vendors feedback

https://www.pcisecuritystandards.org/assessors_and_solutions/ approved_scanning_vendors_feedback

PCI DSS Approved Scanning Vendors

https://www.pcisecuritystandards.org/assessors_and_solutions/ approved_scanning_vendors

This list, which is updated on a regular basis, contains contact details for all approved ASVs. Any ASV that carries out a scan must be on the list when the scan is carried out.

ASV Program Guide v3.1

https://www.pcisecuritystandards.org/documents/ASV_Progra m_Guide_v3.1.pdf?agreement=true&time=1560852761444

This document provides guidance and requirements applicable to ASVs in the framework of the PCI DSS and associated payment brand data protection programmes. Security scanning companies interested in providing scan services as part of the PCI programme must comply with the requirements set out in this document, and must successfully complete the PCI SSC Security Scanning Vendor Testing and Approval Process.

CHAPTER 12: THE PCI DSS AND ISO/IEC 27001

ISO/IEC 27001 is the international information security management standard that more and more organisations are using to ensure that their information security management meets the data protection and compliance requirements of a wide variety of legislation, including the EU's General Data Protection Regulation (GDPR) and the Directive on security of network and information systems (NIS Directive), the US's HIPAA and GLBA, and others.

While the PCI DSS was not written to map specifically to ISO 27001 or to any other existing framework, it sits clearly within the ISO 27001 framework, and organisations that have implemented an ISO 27001 information security management system (ISMS) should be able, with minor additional work, to also demonstrate their conformance with the PCI DSS. The individual controls detailed in the PCI DSS can be mapped to the controls and clauses of ISO 27001 (primarily to Annex A, the list of information security controls).

It certainly makes sense for any organisation that is pursuing either ISO 27001 or PCI DSS compliance, and has both payment card data and other confidential data (whether personally identifiable information – sometimes known as 'PII' – or other commercial information) to protect, to tackle the requirements of the PCI DSS from within the ISO 27001 framework.

CHAPTER 13: THE PAYMENT APPLICATION DATA SECURITY STANDARD (PA-DSS)

The PA-DSS is the PCI SSC-managed programme that focuses on payment applications, such as shopping carts, payment gateways, and so on. This programme was previously run by Visa Inc. and was known as Payment Application Best Practices (PABP). Increasingly, criminals are targeting vulnerabilities in payment applications to steal payment card data, and some users may unknowingly have sensitive card data stored on their systems by software. The PA-DSS is therefore meant to help software vendors and others develop secure payment applications that do not store prohibited data, such as full magnetic stripes, CVV2 or personal identification number (PIN) data, and to ensure their payment applications support compliance with the PCI DSS.

Commercial off-the-shelf (COTS) payment applications that are sold, distributed or licensed to third parties are subject to the PA-DSS requirements. In-house or bespoke payment applications that are developed by merchants or service providers and not sold to a third party are not subject to the PA-DSS requirements, but must still comply with the PCI DSS.

The PA-DSS has its own security audit procedures and its own detailed programme guide[8] that help organisations to determine exactly how these compliance requirements affect them. The PCI SSC also publishes and maintains a list of Validated Payment Applications[9] that have been assessed as having met the requirements of the Standard. As this list is continually updated, we recommend that merchants contact the respective

---

[8]*www.pcisecuritystandards.org/documents/PA-DSS-v3_2-Program-Guide.pdf*.

[9]*www.pcisecuritystandards.org/assessors_and_solutions/vpa_agreement*.

software vendors to confirm that their applications are fully compliant with the latest version of the PA-DSS.

As mentioned in Chapter 6, we strongly recommend the use of a third-party payment gateway service which is fully PCI compliant, particularly for the requirements of a small e-commerce business. While such a service provider is not obliged to use an in-house software application that is compliant with the PA-DSS, we advise that merchants use the larger suppliers that are fully compliant with the PA-DSS and the PCI DSS.

CHAPTER 14: PIN TRANSACTION SECURITY (PTS)

The PCI SSC also has compliance requirements for PIN entry (PIN pad and POS) devices that are used in conjunction with payment cards in environments attended by a cashier, merchant or sales clerk, or those that are unattended, such as garage forecourts. There is a testing and approval guide,[10] together with detailed vendor guidance on how to gain approval. All of this information is available at
www.pcisecuritystandards.org/assessors_and_solutions/pin_transaction_devices.

The PIN Security Requirements contains a complete set of requirements for the secure management, processing and transmission of PIN data during online and offline payment card transaction processing at ATMs, and attended and unattended POS terminals.

The PIN Transaction Security programme includes unattended payment terminals (UPTs) and hardware security modules (HSMs), so that these devices can be rigorously tested to ensure they secure cardholder data in a payment process. UPTs include self-service ticketing machines, kiosks, automated fuel pumps and vending machines. HSMs are secure cryptographic devices that can be used for PIN translation, card personalisation, electronic commerce or data protection and do not include any type of cardholder interface. The PCI SSC maintains a list of approved UPTs and HSMs.

---

[10]*www.pcisecuritystandards.org/documents/PTS_Program_Guide_v1-8.pdf*.

CHAPTER 15: SECURE SOFTWARE STANDARD

The PCI SSC has published standards for the secure design and development of modern payment software. The PCI Secure Software Standard and the PCI Secure Software Lifecycle (Secure SLC) Standard are part of a new PCI Software Security Framework, which includes a validation programme for software vendors and their software products, and a qualification programme for assessors.

The PCI Software Security Standard expands beyond the scope of the PA-DSS for traditional payment software to address overall software security resiliency for modern payment software. Specifically:

- The PCI Secure Software Standard outlines security requirements and assessment procedures to help ensure payment software adequately protects the integrity and confidentiality of payment transactions and data.

- The PCI Secure SLC Standard outlines security requirements and assessment procedures for software vendors to validate how they properly manage the security of payment software throughout the entire software lifecycle.

These standards will replace the PA-DSS when it is retired in 2022. In the meantime, there will be a gradual transition period for organisations with investments in the PA-DSS.

CHAPTER 16: SOFTWARE-BASED PIN ENTRY ON COMMERCIAL OFF-THE-SHELF DEVICES (COTS)

The PCI SSC publishes a standard for software-based PIN entry on COTS devices, such as smartphones and tablets. The PCI Software-Based PIN Entry (SPoC) Standard provides a software-based approach for protecting PIN entry on the wide variety of COTS devices on the market today. The security requirements are for solution providers to use in developing secure solutions that enable EMV contact and contactless transactions with PIN entry on the merchant's consumer device using a secure PIN entry application in combination with a Secure Card Reader for PIN (SCRP).

The Standard comprises two documents – Security Requirements and Test Requirements.

- Security Requirements are objectives for the solution provider that designs the overall solution or components, such as the application that receives the PIN. The Security Requirements can also help other organisations understand expectations for securing these types of payments.

- The Test Requirements create validation mechanisms for payment security laboratories to evaluate the security of a solution. A supporting programme lists PCI-validated software-based PIN entry solutions on the PCI SSC website for merchant use.

FURTHER READING

IT Governance Publishing (ITGP) is the world's leading publisher for governance and compliance. Our industry-leading pocket guides, books, training resources and toolkits are written by real-world practitioners and thought leaders. They are used globally by audiences of all levels, from students to C-suite executives.

Our high-quality publications cover all IT governance, risk and compliance frameworks and are available in a range of formats. This ensures our customers can access the information they need in the way they need it.

Our other publications about information security include:

- *Information Security A Practical Guide* by Tom Mooney, *www.itgovernancepublishing.co.uk/product/information-security-a-practical-guide*
- *Nine Steps to Success: An ISO 27001:2013 Implementation Overview* by Alan Calder *www.itgovernancepublishing.co.uk/product/nine-steps-to-success*
- *The Psychology of Information Security* by Leron Zinatullin *www.itgovernancepublishing.co.uk/product/the-psychology-of-information-security*

For more information on ITGP and branded publishing services, and to view our full list of publications, please visit *www.itgovernancepublishing.co.uk*.

To receive regular updates from ITGP, including information on new publications in your area(s) of interest, sign up for our newsletter at *www.itgovernancepublishing.co.uk/topic/newsletter*.

Branded publishing

Through our branded publishing service, you can customise ITGP publications with your company's branding. Find out more at

www.itgovernancepublishing.co.uk/topic/branded-publishing-services.

Related services

ITGP is part of GRC International Group, which offers a comprehensive range of complementary products and services to help organisations meet their objectives.

For a full range of PCI DSS resources, please visit *www.itgovernance.co.uk/pci_dss*.

Training services

The IT Governance training programme is built on our extensive practical experience designing and implementing management systems based on ISO standards, best practice and regulations.

Our courses help attendees develop practical skills and comply with contractual and regulatory requirements. They also support career development via recognised qualifications.

Learn more about our training courses and view the full course catalogue at

www.itgovernance.co.uk/training.

Professional services and consultancy

We are a leading global consultancy of IT governance, risk management and compliance solutions. We advise businesses around the world on their most critical issues and present cost-saving and risk-reducing solutions based on international best practice and frameworks.

We offer a wide range of delivery methods to suit all budgets, timescales and preferred project approaches.

Find out how our consultancy services can help your organisation at *www.itgovernance.co.uk/consulting*.

Industry news

Want to stay up to date with the latest developments and resources in the IT governance and compliance market? Subscribe to our Weekly Round-up newsletter and we will send you mobile-friendly emails with fresh news and features about your preferred areas of interest, as well as unmissable offers and free resources to help you successfully start your project: *www.itgovernance.co.uk/weekly-round-up*.